INTERNATIONAL COUNCIL
ON ARCHIVES

CONSEIL INTERNATIONAL
DES ARCHIVES

ICA Handbooks Series
Volume 8

The Management of Business Records

by
Anna Christina Ulfsparre

K·G·Saur
München · New York · London · Paris 1988

CIP-Titelaufnahme der Deutschen Bibliothek

The management of business records / ed. Christina Ulfsparre.
– München ; New York ; London ; Paris : Saur, 1988
(ICA handbooks series ; Vol. 8)
ISBN 3-598-20280-6
NE: Ulfsparre, Christina [Hrsg.]; International Council on Archives:
ICA handbooks series

Copyright 1988 by K.G. Saur Verlag GmbH & Co KG, München
(A member of the international Butterworths Group, London)
Printed in the Federal Republic of Germany

Photocomposition by Fotosatz Herbert Buck, 8300 Kumhausen
Printed by Strauß Offsetdruck, 6945 Hirschberg 2
ISBN 3-598-20280-6

CONTENTS

PREFACE

The content of this manual was discussed at the annual meeting of the Business Archives Committee held in Madrid in 1987. All the members of the committee have made very helpful suggestions and useful alterations and additions. The chairwoman Dr. Hilda Coppejans-Desmedt has read the manuscript and made important comments on the text. The British member of the committee, Mrs. Lesley Richmond had an essential mission, to correct and revise the language. Apart from this unenviable work, Mrs. Richmond has made useful comments and additions, especially in Chapter 4 on storage and in Chapter 5 on repair and conservation.

Chapter 1

RECORDS AND ARCHIVAL MANAGEMENT
GENERAL APPROACH

1. INTRODUCTION

It is often said that an archive is superfluous to a company's or a firm's requirements. On the contrary, it can be stated that a company needs its records and that an archive is not a luxury. Companies require many different kinds of information, much of which can be provided by their own records. However, the reasons for preserving records are not only administrative and related to the actual running of a company, they can also provide a company with a history. If a company does not have a history it lacks a corporate identity with which managers, employees and customers can associate.

Taking a wider view it can also be said that business forms an essential part of economic history and that the bond between companies and society is important. There is also a correlation between the business community, whether private or public, and the public administration, whether local or national. It can, therefore, be argued that it is good business management to have a well kept archive.

Sooner or later the archival and records management tasks of a business have to be tackled. A large company will have to meet these problems from the outset, while a small company can afford to ignore them for decades. The problems are often never faced until it is time to write the company's history. Then, the company's archives are placed in the foreground and the problems of records and archival management are highlighted. However, by that time, many vital records may have been destroyed. It will be stated, again and again, that a well organized and arranged archive saves time and money.

The present development in office management with the rapidly increasing use of micro-computers and programs for many office routines, which were previously dealt with by hand, means that the problems of information handling cannot be avoided. We have witnessed a rapid increase in the amount of information recorded on paper in recent years. The peak may have already been reached as the computerized offices of the 1990s will probably create less paper. However, less paper does not mean less documentation as the same amount of information will continue to be produced. Information produced and handled by EDP equipment and by telecommunication will constitute most of what the archivist and records manager will have to face in the future.

The modern office, large and small, is becoming an electronic environment and this means that strict rules are required for the handling, filing, retention and disposal of records (records by definition include magnetic mediums, films, etc.). Another important point is that changes in personnel demand a systematized flow of records. New members of staff must be able to become familiar rapidly with their jobs and to deal efficiently with their tasks. Changes in production and operation may also create demands for more efficient control of records and flow of information.

However, in order to decide which records are to be retained and kept for posterity, it is essential to know what records exist and, if possible, how they are related. The first step, therefore, is to make an inventory[1] of the records. Such an inventory should reflect provenance in its description of the scope and content of the records.

2. PREPARING AND PRODUCING A RECORDS SURVEY OR ARCHIVAL INVENTORY

2.1 DESCRIPTION OF THE ORGANISATION

In order to establish the flow of information within a business, it is necessary to get a clear picture of its organisation. An organisational chart may need to be drawn up if one does not already exist. It is often the case within a business that procedures outlive their usefulness but no one has the interest, time or energy to discover whether they could be revised or abolished. When archival problems are tackled and a chart of the organisation is compiled, indications often appear of ways to rationalize old procedures. An important part of rationalization within a business involves the systematic control of its records, the ordering of its archives, and the simplification of office routines.

In conclusion, the first step is to obtain a proper picture of the organisation of the firm, as this will provide an overview of office routines. The next step is to make a physical inventory of the records of the firm, including those produced by EDP and telecommunication equipment.

2.2 INVENTORIES

It is assumed here that one company is the creator of the records, i.e. the provenance is tied to that company, and thus one archive group (called record group in the

---

1. An inventory is a finding aid listing and describing in varying degrees of detail the contents of one or more record/archive groups, fonds, classes or series, usually including a brief history of the organisation and functions of the originating firm/s and if appropriate, indices. Dictionary of Archival Terminology, ICA Handbook Series, vol 3, 1984.

U.S.A.) is formed.[2] The possibility that the archives of one company may contain the records of many other companies, which have evolved from or have been absorbed by the original company, will not be taken into consideration at the moment.[3]

When preparing an inventory the organisational chart should be followed, proceeding from one division to the next. Small companies are often not organized in divisions and in such cases the inventory should follow functions. It is advisable to work in close connection with the people who create the records and those responsible for general service and supply. At a later stage, it will be necessary to contact the company's financial and legal experts in order to safeguard and support the appraisal of the records.

The creation of records, in this context, is defined as being attached to its provenance (origin, creator). In a company which is organized in divisions, each division can be looked upon as a separate creator of its records. Even a function such as senior management can be a separate creator of records. It is convenient to begin an inventory with the records located in the company's office and then proceed to deal with those records which have been transferred to other storage areas such as records centres and archives. Usually the same type of records can be found in either locality, i.e. records from the current year and the year before in the office and older ones in the records centre/archive. Careful consideration as to the age at which records are transferred from "current" to "non current" use can help ease storage problems by creating space and facilities in the office. A suitable timetable for the transfer of records to the records centre or archive will be economical in other ways, e.g. the records can be moved from expensive storage containers to cheap storage boxes.

2.3 THE DESCRIPTION OF THE RECORDS/ARCHIVES

The records should be identified and described by their function, subject, arrangement or some other common characteristic. Thus they will form different units, called records series.[4] Examples of different series include ledgers, minutes and files[5] arranged according to a filing plan/system[6].

The minimum requirement when drawing up an inventory is that the records series is described correctly. It is also important to give correct, clear and unambiguous descriptions. These descriptions should be used when storage boxes are marked or labelled. This will facilitate record retrieval, appraisal and disposal. If unskilled personnel are to undertake retrieval, it is essential that the labelling is clear. This is also of great importance when the appraisal and evaluation of the records is carried out as correct descriptions are a requirement for reaching sound decisions.

---

2. Archive group is defined as the primary division in the arrangement of archives at the level of the independent originating unit or agency. Record group is defined as a body of organisationally and functionally related records established on the basis of provenance with particular regard to the administrative history, complexity and quantity of the records, archives of the agency, institution or organisation involved. Dictionary of Archival Terminology, ICA Handbook Series, vol 3, 1984.
3. See pages 63 ff. where research and historical archives are discussed.

The labels should contain information about the name, division, records series, dates covered, the number of the item(s) and, where necessary, the date for destruction.

Figure 1

Smith & Co, Ltd	
Copies of invoices	
(Type of series/record)	
1984	
(Year/period/series)	
G 3 A (Records series)	
1995	
(Date for destruction)	

Smith & Co, Ltd
Copies of invoices
(Type of series/records)
1984   (Year/period)
No 275 – 350 (Invoice no.)
G 3 A (Records series)
1995
(Date for destruction)
Finance Department
(Issuing division/function)

The following identifiers are required to describe a records series:

1. The name of the firm and division

A records series will *always* have to be identified as belonging to the creator of the records/archives, i.e. a company or a division within it, such as the purchase division, the general service office, etc. Other descriptions for the creator of the records are "fond" or "record group"[7]. The ties between the creator of the records and the records series are of great importance when distinguishing between different archives/fonds/archive groups created by the buying and selling of businesses and company amalgamations. The possibility of future sales, purchases and mergers always have to be considered. This also applies to internal changes such as the formation of new divisions or functions, or the closure of old ones.

2. The name of the series

The name of the records series should clearly indicate its content and function.

---

4. A (record) series consists of items or documents arranged in accordance with a filing plan/system or maintained as a unit because they relate to a particular function or subject, result from the same activity, have a particular form or because of some other relationship arising out of the circumstances of their creation or use. Dictionary of Archival Terminology, ICA Handbook Series, vol 3, 1984

5. A file is an organised unit of documents grouped together either for current use or in the process of archival arrangement. Dictionary of Archival Terminology, ICA Handbook Series, vol 3, 1984.

6. A filing plan/system is a predetermined classification plan for the physical arrangement, storage and retrieval of files, usually identified by the type of symbols used e.g. alphabetical, numerical, alpha-numerical, decimal. Dictionary of Archival Terminology, ICA Handbook Series, vol 3, 1984

7. *Fonds* is defined as the total body of records/archives accumulated by a particular individual, institution or organisation in the exercise of its activities and functions.

3. The covering dates of the series

The opening and the closing dates of the records series should be given.

4. The retention period and storage location

When compiling an inventory of the records, the existing retention periods and location of the records series should be recorded. Thought should also be given as to the retention and disposal of records not yet appraised.

5. The number of units/volumes[8] in the series

This information is useful for planning storage facilities and calculating the annual growth of the records. The quantity should be given in linear metres.

6. The name of the creator of the records[9]

This is of importance when deciding how the records should be kept, and if and when they are to be destroyed.

An example of an inventory is given below:

Figure 2 A

Company		Inventory list		
Name of the company/division/function				
Record series	Period Begin/end	Storage Where no of years	No of volumes	Remarks
Minutes etc	1937 – 76	Strongroom	3	1938 is lost

Figure 2 B

Company			Inventory					
Item no	Name of file/ records	Opening date	Closing date	Form	Original code	Storage period	Retention period	Remarks
3	Minutes	1937	1976	Bound	–	Strong room	–	1938 is lost

8. The unit/volume can either be a ring binder or a box or loose papers kept together with a string
9. The creator can be a department, a division, an enterprise, a person, etc.

More ambitious inventories can also include:
- an estimation of the total linear metreage of records in the office, and their annual growth
- an investigation of the structure of the present and past filing plan/systems (if they exist)
- a summary of what is filed in the present filing plan/systems
- a record of the frequency with which documents are retrieved on a monthly or annual basis
- a survey of the level of document reproduction

If a more detailed list of records is to be made, it may be appropriate to use inventory cards. These can be sorted according to different criteria, such as records series or record groups.

Figure 3: Inventory cards

Responsible Creator:		Classification No:		Heading
Type of Record: Organized by function ☐ File organized ☐				
Sorting order: Alphabetically: ☐ Chronologically: ☐ Numerically: ☐ Other: ☐				
Stored in: Binders: ☐ Boxes: ☐ Cabinet drawers: ☐ Other: ☐				
Storage place and years: Office: ☐ Years: Records Centre: ☐ Years: Archive: ☐ Years:				
Starting year	No of items	Inventory date	Inventory signature	Archival notes (Transfer date, Disposal year etc)
		Office notes:		
Shelf metre	Annual growth	Date of approval	Signature	

The use of a word processor in the compilation of an inventory simplifies sorting and is an excellent tool for the job. Naturally, if a filing plan/system is in use within a company, it should be consulted when the inventory is compiled.

It is to be remembered that compiling cards or lists is undertaken in the same way whether the records are kept in archival storage, located in the office or stored elsewhere. There is no difference between records kept in the office and those stored in the archive or records centre. All records must be appraised and dealt with in the same manner.

2.4 HOW TO COMPILE AN INVENTORY

The crucial problem is to decide who is to carry out the job. It must be a person with the correct qualifications and it is essential to make it clear to management that it is *not* a task to hand out to the youngest office boy. Knowledge about the organisation of the company is very important and, if possible, also something about its history. Interest in records management and filing and a systematic, organized mind, able to analyse the flow of records are also of importance. Individual companies may require other qualifications. Some companies will already have a specialist, such as an archivist or a records manager on their payroll and others may decide to call in an expert.

When the inventory is being compiled, it is advisable to follow the organisation of the company using an organisational chart. The inventory will then be automatically set up according to the functions and operations of the company and records will be naturally grouped together in series and sub-series. This will also reveal the reason why different records series have been created. For instance, a main record series group like accounting records may contain ledgers as one sub-series, balance sheets as another and so forth, and so a hierarchical structure is thus formed.

Compiling an inventory will often reveal a natural order in records/archives which should not be altered.

In many businesses the following record series will be found: minutes, correspondence (both in-letters and copies of out-letters), share registers, legal, financial, and, statistical records, etc.

Sometimes only the above mentioned documents exist in the main record series, but in the majority of companies the creation of records is more complex and the main records series must be divided in sub-series. The accounting records series is usually subdivided into many sub-series, eg. ledgers, cash accounts, memorandum books, cost specification books, purchase and sales accounts, invoices, etc. Minutes can be subdivided into meetings of the board of directors, of working groups, of annual meetings, etc., and correspondence can be subdivided into letters filed alphabetically, chronologically or by other criteria − by subject, administratively by clients, etc.

Finally, it should also be pointed out, that compiling an inventory is a good aid and natural starting point for the formation of a more advanced records management/archival system. How advanced a system is required, has to be decided for each firm individually. The inventory, however, must always include additional information with rules for retention, disposal and destruction.

3. APPRAISAL, RETENTION, DISPOSAL AND DESTRUCTION

3.1 RETENTION SCHEDULES

The control of the current records in a company is not only a problem for management. The appraisal/evaluation of the future worth of records is an essential and fundamental concern of archivists and records managers, especially those with the care of large collections of twentieth century records. Which records should be retained and kept for posterity? Which records should be destroyed and when should the destruction take place? A schedule for the retention and disposal of records has to be established. This process of determining and stating in a records schedule the appropriate retention period and ultimate disposal date of a record series is called scheduling and the records so processed are called scheduled records.

The records schedule is based on information from the inventory list or cards. The accuracy of the initial inventory and the description of the records series is vital to the next stage, an analysis of the series. The series is analysed in order to devise an appropriate retention schedule, which will meet the current administrative, fiscal and legal requirements and to ensure the proper disposal of the records. The retention/disposal schedule and the inventory will together form a Records Creation Plan (RCP) i.e. a plan for the processing (handling), filing, storing, retention and destruction of records. The filing plan/system forms a part of the RCP.

A detailed RCP assumes that the record holdings are surveyed one more time. If a decision has been made that some records series require a final review, then it must stated when this will happen, the procedure to be followed and the personnel required for its implementation.

Figure 4: Example of a Records Creation Plan

Name of the company					
Function: Administration and Finance			Approved 23/05/1987	Issued 01/07/87	
Record	Record description	Storage period			Remarks
series		Office	Archive	Destruction	
F 1	Property Records	10 y	Ever	–	
F 5	Sales Prognosis	1 y	3 y	4 y	Since 1985, on line

3.2 RULES FOR DISPOSAL AND DESTRUCTION

It is important to form fixed rules for the retention, disposal and destruction of the records. The Records Creation Plan (RCP) must include information about the retention period prior to the destruction of records and must state which records should be retained for posterity.

There is a tendency to arbitrarily set retention periods of ten years for all records. In many countries, this is based on the legal requirements for the retention of certain records. However, the legal and administrative requirements for each group of records should be carefully investigated and accurate retention periods set. In many cases routine records can be destroyed after two, three or five years.

The feasibility for the disposal and the destruction of records must be constantly reviewed.

It is recommended that the records to be destroyed and those to be retained should be kept apart and, if possible, they should form separate records series. The separation should be done as soon as practicality allows and the destruction of the records should be carried out regularly, ideally at the beginning of each year. The procedure will of course involve records stored in the office, in the records centre and in the archive.

It is recommended that a check is made to ensure that records designated for destruction are actually destroyed. This is important for reasons of security, safety and confidence.

4. MAKING A GUIDE TO THE ARCHIVE

4.1 THE VALUE OF A GUIDE

An inventory with rules for retention, disposal and destruction or a records creation plan is in many cases, a sufficient aid to control the flow of records and to ensure efficient retrieval. However, it may be useful to produce a special guide to those records which are to be retained and kept for the future, as the "historical" archival holding will certainly make up only a small part of the total. Such a guide will prove invaluable when the records of the company are to be used to compile a public relations pamphlet, write the history of the company or describe the operation and development of the business in some other context.

Many companies may benefit from a guide covering all the records and not only the "historical" archive. In such a case, the inventory and the records creation plan must be further developed and extended.

4.2 RULES FOR MAKING A GUIDE

The first rule for making a guide to the records of a business is to discover whether the records have been created by one company or by several companies. The parent company and its subsidiaries must be distinguished from each other according to the principle of provenance. If one company has bought another, the records of the purchased company should be listed in a separate section. Each company is considered to be one unit. The situation when a company changes its name, when production alters, when parts are bought and sold, all pose problems when producing a guide.

The records of a company organised in divisions (sections) should be listed in the guide separately by division. The company's organisation is then followed as in the inventory or records creation plan. As has already been stated, the creator of the records can either be a company, or a division or function of that company.

The records should be arranged in the archival guide in the same way as they were in the records creation plan, i.e. in separate series and sub-series, with items listed within the series.

It does not matter in which form the records are created. It is not important whether a cash book is kept manually, with the help of an accounting machine, or by computer. The importance lies in its function of being a cash book.

There are exceptions for practical reasons. Due to their format, maps, drawings, photographs and cinematographic films are listed *per se* in separate series and not according to their function or content. Maps and drawings are further discussed on page 39 ff. and photographs and cinematographic films on page 40 ff.

5. SUMMARY

Without a records creation plan companies run a great risk of retaining records for longer than required and storing them uneconomically, both of which incur unneccessary expense. Badly planned and unsystematic records and archival management will inevitably lead to an overflow in the office and/or archival storage. The decision may then be made to create space by destroying records arbitrarily. This may prove very expensive in the short, as well as in the long run, because important records may be lost as a result.

Thoughtless and unplanned weeding and destruction of records may cost large sums of money in carrying out new record surveys and trying to reconstruct information and documentation. If rules are not established for the length of time of retention and place of storage, uncertainty will occur as to the location of and the survival of the records themselves. There are very good reasons for the compilation of a records inventory and a records management system. Retrieval time is shortened, space is used economically and records are destroyed with no fear of damage to the business.

The motives for keeping an historical archive have already been stressed, but it can also be pointed out, that businesses do not need to fear that keeping records for future research is an expensive responsibility. The cost of maintaining an historical archive is not large. If the records and archival management problems have been tackled and an inventory with a records retention schedule or a records creation plan has been compiled, then it will have been shown that the historical records do not form more than a few per cent of the annual production of the records within a company.

Minimum Work To Be Carried Out

1. Make an inventory of the records
2. Decide on the retention period for every type of record and add a retention/disposal schedule to the inventory list
3. Destroy the records scheduled for destruction
4. Transfer non-current records to special records or archival storage areas. These records should then be stored in labelled boxes.
5. Make a guide of the archives

Chapter 2

FILE DOCUMENTATION AND SEARCH SYSTEMS

1. INTRODUCTION

In the previous chapter the methods of introducing basic order into business records and establishing rules and guidelines for control over their growth, management and final storage were discussed. However, these measures are not always sufficient. The quantity of records and the company's size, organization, existing office premises and records management procedures may demand more thorough file organization, management and retrieval.

2. FILE ORGANIZATION OR THE CREATION OF A FILING PLAN/SYSTEM

2.1 FLOW CHARTS

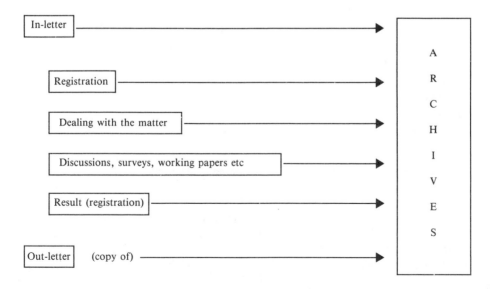

All these stages will lead to the creation of records. A schedule for file organization and a records management plan are suitable starting points for a thorough description of how records are used and how they are transferred between sections and eventually to the records centre or archive. Flow charts showing the systematic movement of records within a company are most useful. The flow chart shows:

1. where the record has been created within the company or where it has been received from outside
2. which functions, sections or divisions will take action and deal with the matter
3. who is responsible for the reports or summing up and consequently the final decision and measures to be taken.

Thus, flow charts are efficient instruments for regulating files, leading to the formation of a registry system. Documents are controlled and processed and an overview of where records are located at any given time is acquired.

Flow charts have to be adjusted to the organization and needs of different companies. These charts are aids, not means in themselves, and they are useful complements to the organizational plans of a company.

Flow charts also form an important base of information from which to decide that certain records are to be destroyed and help confirm disposal schedules. If it is known why records exist, how they are managed, and who is responsible for them, then it is possible to act quickly when destruction is due.

2.2 FORMS

A form is defined as
1) a document, printed or otherwise produced, with pre-designated spaces for the recording of specified information or
2) a document intended to serve as a model

Forms are common aids in office work composing a large part of the paper flow. They influence the daily work and the routine of both records and archival management.

Forms, according to their function, can either be administrative or operational.

Administrative forms may
manage
describe
inform
summarize/analyse
control

They can for example, be used for summoning meetings, for planning and for describing judgements, statements and statistical and financial reports.

Forms produced by an office include orders, applications tenders and offers.

Administrative forms are used as a management tool and affect routines and activities while office forms hold information which is in itself operational. The quantity of forms used by a business makes it necessary to know, from the beginning, the purpose for which the forms are used, who will use them and the kind of information that they hold. Once these facts have been established, it will be possible to evaluate their place within the total flow of records and their future, i.e. retention or destruction. Non-current forms ought to be removed from office storage on a regular basis.

It can be clearly seen that the control of forms is a very important part of creating an efficient flow of records within a company.

2.3 TRANSFER OF RECORDS TO A RECORDS CENTRE OR ARCHIVE

A pre-requisite of good records management is that there are fixed rules for the transfer of records. When a record becomes non-current, it should be sent to a records centre/limbo storage or an archive and stored according to guidelines drawn up for records and archive management. The way in which the transfer is carried out will depend on the required length of time that any record has to be immediately accessible and the type and location of storage areas.

Special records storage areas can be located close to working areas, e.g. storage stacks in each department or division, managed by that department or division. In other cases, a central records store may serve the whole company. In most cases a company's central records store also houses the company's archive, as only large companies operate both a records centre or limbo storage and an archive.

Where a company operates a filing plan/system, it will also maintain record storage in the office. Filing then takes place as soon as the matter concerned is dealt with. The transfer of files[1] to the records centre or the archive will be carried out according to fixed rules. Correct filing presupposes a fixed filing system.

The greater the distance between the office and the allocated records storage area, the greater the risk that the records will remain too long in the office, causing files and filing storage to overflow and the transfer of files to records storage to be delayed unnecessarily.

Premises and storage equipment create natural limits to the amount of records it is possible to keep and store in offices. It is easy to estimate the quantity of records dealt with during one year and to calculate how many years of records can be stored in any given office area. Thus, the longest possible storage time can be calculated and the date for the transfer of records can be fixed.

However, storage capacity should not be a guideline to the length of time records are to be kept in an office area. Most records loose their currency quickly and there is no need to keep them in expensive office space when they are not required. It is necessary to create a system for file transfer, which is based on such facts as the usage, the currency and the archival value of the records, and not on such matters as the location and size of storage. A registry system can control the creation and maintenance of current and semi-current files through the use of a filing plan. The transfer of files to the records centre, limbo storage or archive should be annual,

---

1. Files are defined as a collective term frequently applied to part or all of the records of an agency. Here it is applied to *part* of the records, i.e. the records arranged according to subjects; thus minutes, accounts, diaries, registers etc. are not considered to be files.

triennial, quinquennial or decennial. The period between file transfers is dependent on the size, growth and use of the files.

When a company's archive repository is located at a distance from its office, it may be practical to operate an intermediate storage area, e.g. a records centre or limbo storage for semi-current records and file storage. File organisation in intermediate storage is the same as that operated in the office. Records kept in intermediate storage are transferred to the archive at the same time as those kept in an office.

The filing plan/system itself does not set the time for file transfer. This will depend on the type of records, how they have been kept, arranged or filed and their currency. Appraisal of the files/records will have taken place and resulted in the designation of the files into those to be kept for posterity and those to be destroyed eventually. The filing plan/system may include special rules for final filing in the archive repository. The records may have to be re-arranged in a series before being registered in the archival guide. The arrangement within a series of preserved files may therefore differ from the order that existed in the office.

Before a file is closed, it is wise to weed it, i.e. to examine it and remove scraps of paper and notes of no obvious value and duplicate copies of documents. Weeding files is relatively easy when filing and closing of files is carried out chronologically and not based on a classification plan, as it is comparatively easy to decide how long records are required for daily work. In- and out-letters series usually have a current value for 3 – 5 years. It does not matter, whether they are kept together in a correspondence series or kept separated in an in-letter- and an out-letter series. In some companies extra copies of out-letters are kept in a separate series but generally such copies are only of use during the current year and consequently they can be destroyed at the end of that year.

The currency of accounts is dependent on the book keeping and auditing system used. This often means that after two years they can be transferred out of the office but not, of course, destroyed, as generally financial legislation demands a much longer period of retention. Statistics are normally of interest for only a short period of time and can be transferred to less expensive records storage after a couple of years.

If the records have been sorted and arranged in files according to a classification scheme, it is often more cumbersome and difficult to evaluate their current usefulness and, therefore, the date for their transfer to a records centre, limbo storage or archive. Records which belong to homogeneous, chronologically arranged series can be transferred as non-current files as soon as they have reached their specified age. When transferring records filed according to a filing plan, it is necessary to review the whole system and decide which files containing records dating prior to a certain year are to be stored in the office and which are not. The latter can be put in labelled boxes and transferred to the records centre, limbo storage or archive. The labels on the boxes should contain classification number plus, possibly, the content, the covering dates of the records and the destruction date where applicable. The review/check and the file transfer have to be carried out annually or every 3 – 10 years, depending on the size and complexity of the filing system.

It is important that the storage and transfer of the records from the office to their final storage or destruction is dealt with in accordance with set rules and that good order is maintained at all levels. The rules must be enforced for all records without consideration to their frequency of retrieval or value. The arrangement of the records on the shelves should be as clear and easy as possible and the labels distinct and informative.

If a records or archival management plan exists together with a filing plan/system, the arrangement of the records both in the office and in archival storage should be based on that plan. If it is carried through systematically, the employees of the company will become accustomed to good order and they will be able to find their way more easily around each other's working areas and in the records storage area.

3. SEARCH SYSTEMS

3.1 ALPHABETICAL, NUMERICAL AND GEOGRAPHICAL PRINCIPLES

Every office requires a system for the arrangement of current records. Such a filing plan/system can be based on various principles, the choice depending on the type of record.

Alphabetical order is simple, straightforward, and at the same time, a very practical solution for arranging certain types of documents, e.g. correspondence. The records or letters are sorted by the name of the receiver or the sender. (NB Existing rules for alphabetical sorting have to be followed)

Numerical order is often suitable for accounts, such as receipts, invoices, etc. Many companies have built up complicated numerical systems for these types or records. For instance, invoices may be numbered in such a manner that the first two figures indicate the place, the next three the customer or client and so on.

Neither the alphabetical nor the numerical order demands special indexes to facilitate retrieval.

Geographical order is often used to separate activity by place or district. The system is based on the fact that geographical areas can be split into smaller areas. Within the smallest unit individuals, firms and institutions are sorted alphabetically. The order consists of country, district, place, name of person or firm.

Example of geographical order
   The county of Cambridge
     Ely (town)
       Caldwell (company)
       Findus   (firm within the company)
       Jones   (individual)
       . . .
       Smith (individual)
   The county of Essex
       . . .

3.2 THE FILING PLAN/SYSTEM AND CLASSIFICATION SYSTEM

If a simple system is rational and efficient there is no need to make it more complicated, but in some cases it is necessary to use more advanced methods. This may happen when the type of records and their contents are so diverse that it is impossible to keep them together using numerical or geographical principles. Serveral documents concerning a similar subject will be kept together in one file and so many records with different origins relating to the same subject will then come together and form files. Thus, records concerning the same subject are linked and furthermore, files from different sources but covering the same subject are also linked. A specific plan is produced, based on the classification of the documents, in order to organize and systematize their filing and retrieval.

Records concerning the same subject should be kept together. The headings of the subjects and, where applicable, the subheadings will be given a set of numbers or letters or a combination of the two. This classification number is noted on the document itself. Thus, records or documents relating to the same subject will be based on an evaluation of the content of the record or document.

Large companies and institutions have extensive and complicated filing systems designed for their own special requirements. As the management and the function of every company is unique, it is rare for the filing plan/system of one company to be operable by another without alterations being made to it.

As it has already been pointed out, there are several types of filing plans and registry systems. Generally they are built up logically and hierarchically, proceeding from the main heading to the sub-headings. It is also possible to use a combination of the numerical and alphabetical systems, producing an alphanumerical system. In such cases the main groups are given alphabetical references and the subheadings numerical ones.

Example:
    Prop = Property
    O   = General issues
    1   = The area of the main factory
    2   = The rest of the country
    3   = Europe
    4   = Overseas

It is possible to use references which are arranged alphabetically after the first letter or the first two or three letters of a keyword. It is, of course, also possible to consider a combination of alphabetically arranged subject headings and within these, alphabetically arranged references. In such cases the system is not hierarchical because it does not presuppose any division or subdivision between groups.

Example:
    Fi = Finance
    Brighton
    Cambridge
    Edinburgh
    . . .

Pe = Personnel

. . .

Pro = Production

A common numerical system is based on division by tenths. Ten main headings (0-9) are divided into ten sub-headings (00-09), and those can then be sub-divided into further sub-headings like 000-009 and so forth.

Example:
    0 = Management and Organisation
      00 = General issues
      01 = Legal matters
      . . .

    1 = Personnel
      10 = General issues
      11 = Agreements
      12 = Employment
      . . .
      18 = Training and information

Before starting to construct a filing plan/system, it has to be decided whether it is to be in force and used by the whole company or if it is be structured for each division or section.

The choice of system will depend on the management and organization of the company and its business activities. It is impossible to recommend a system but a succesful one must have the following qualities:

— be easy to understand
— allow easy retrieval
— provide control over the records
— be flexible
— be adaptable to future decisions about retention and disposal
— correspond to current office procedures and legislation

The construction of a filing plan/system demands a very through study of the management and the organisation of a company. It is important to define the aims, subjects and subject areas very clearly and to give them unambiguous headings. Misunderstanding and confusion must be avoided if the system is to function successfully.

Documentation from projects consist of records which are linked to a specially defined scheme/project. Special groups of people are chosen to work together in a certain project. Project records are created along side those normally resulting from the activities of the company. When a project begins it is advisable to inform the project team about the demands of documentation and subsequently, during the time of the project, to consider possible adjustments or additions. The records from a project will include printed reports, routine descriptions, drawings, instructions and literature as well as administrative records. All these records should be kept together and be classified and registered in a suitable way, i.e. according to the project number or project index.

The computer can substantially aid records management when a filing plan/system is in use. However, the method, whether it be manual or computerized, chosen for processing the filing plan/system will not affect the logic and substance of that system.

Chapter 3

RECORDS RENTENTION

1. REASONS FOR RECORDS RETENTION

1.1. ADMINISTRATIVE AND MANAGEMENT REQUIREMENTS

The need for certain information to serve a company's own administration is a primary reason to retain records. Records are necessary for the management of personnel and the instruction and training of employees. Other records are essential for policy making and to gain information about clients and customers. Records can also contain proof of the existence of certain rights and privileges, while others contain valuable technical information − these can be long-lived. Many more examples can be cited. It can also be argued that knowledge of a company's history, provided by its records, is of value to its managers and employees. The analysis of long term changes can give both managers and employees a better insight into present problems and be of guidance to the future management of the company.

1.1.1. The administrative and management viewpoint

In the first instance consideration must be given as to whether records are subject to any legal restrictions, such as those relating to the organisation of companies; the protection of employees and the environment; accounts and taxes; insurance; data protection and security.

However, when records appraisal is carried out, it is not only the legal requirements for the retention of records, which have to be taken into consideration but also the administrative needs of the business. For what length of time is the information required? This will naturally depend on the nature of a company's business. For example, companies producing capital equipment with a long life expectancy require to retain certain records in order to deal with repairs, requests for spare parts, etc.

The frequency of use of the records, i.e. the daily or weekly need for them and the volume, "the physical bulk", of record series also need to be taken into account during record appraisal in order that the records can be managed in the most economical way. Consideration will also need to be given as to the benefit which will arise when records are transferred from expensive storage in easily accessible office premises to less accessible "cheap" archival stacks or direct destruction.

Some records may be of interest to the management of a company for quite a short period of time compared with that required by laws and other regulations. It is not advisable, however, to destroy all records as soon as the required legal retention period is completed. Consideration must also be given to the historical value of the records for public relations, for the history of the company and for research in general.

1.2. HISTORICAL RESEARCH

Another reason to retain and keep records is to provide present and future researchers with historical source material. It is in the interest of a business to make its records available for research. If the historians and researchers, who are to write the history of a company or describe and analyse certain events in the business world, are not given access to the records of the business itself, they will have to use official records such as government investigations and legal and tax records. These records can give only a limited picture and will often only shed light upon a business when it is in trouble and close to bankruptcy. Such an approach has been likened to describing a marriage with the help of divorce records. The account of the development of the company, its management and influence, will be partial and incomplete.

A company may have influenced technical and economic development both in its own local area and nationwide, and have also influenced the social development of individuals. The chairmen and managing directors of companies have often played an important part both in local and national affairs. Concern for the environment is currently very topical but to study this important subject, access must be gained to business records in order to judge and evaluate the technical, social and economic influence of companies.

External users of a company's records have little knowledge about its organisation and require guidance and help. Documents not only need to be produced on request, they need to be presented within a clear context with preceding and/or related documents; in other words the material should be "documentally available".[1]

1.3. PUBLICITY OR PUBLIC RELATIONS

Public relations work often demands access to different types of records, old and new. There is large public interest in the way in which companies act and develop, and it is to be expected that this interest will increase in the future. Knowledge and insight about the development of a company and its management will make it possible to demonstrate its social and economic operations. The operations of a company influence both individuals, groups of people and institutions and so the overall planning and policy of the government of any country demands knowledge and information about the management and strategy of various companies.

---

1. This has been pointed out by Mr Chris Jansen, Philips

1.3.1. The public relations (PR) and research value of business records

Records which are required for academic research will also be of value to a company, when the time comes to document its own development. However, the managing director of a company or an owner of a business may think that records which throw light upon an embarassing incident or indicate mismanagement should be destroyed. Academic researchers do not, of course, accept such a policy and will argue with managers and owners, that a full and complete version of the company's history is essential and is advantageous to the company. Top management must be convinced that it is much better to protect sensitive information from unauthorized access than to destroy it. Special rules for access and storage can be applied to records containing this type of information.

When the history of a company is to be written, it is advisable that access is given to records dealing with administrative and operational procedures plus important internal and external correspondence, including the papers and correspondence of the managing director, the board of directors and other personnel. Access to ledgers, annual balance sheets and accounts, personnel lists, salary lists, contracts, deals, agreements and similar records will also be required.

It is advisable to retain all the surviving records of the first few years of a company's life. These are usually very few in number and are very useful, not only for research, but also for exhibitions, etc.

1.4. VITAL RECORDS

When compiling the inventory and the records creation plan many records will be classified as vital to the company. These are records which would ensure the continuation of the business in the event of a disaster. These records should be stored securely (in a safe or vault) having regard to the risk of fire, flooding and burglary. The quantity of such records is generally very small.

It is also important that valuable documents and drawings are microfilmed or copied in some way and that the original and the copy are stored in different locations. A list of the duplicated documents should always be compiled.

The following is a list of the types of information about a company which should be preserved permanently for historical purposes.[2]

---

2. See "Weeding and Selection in the Philips Archives" by Mr Chris Jansen, published in *Bulletin* of the Business Archives Committee of the International Council of Archives, no 9. The list is published here with the consent of Mr Jansen, from whom copies may be obtained.

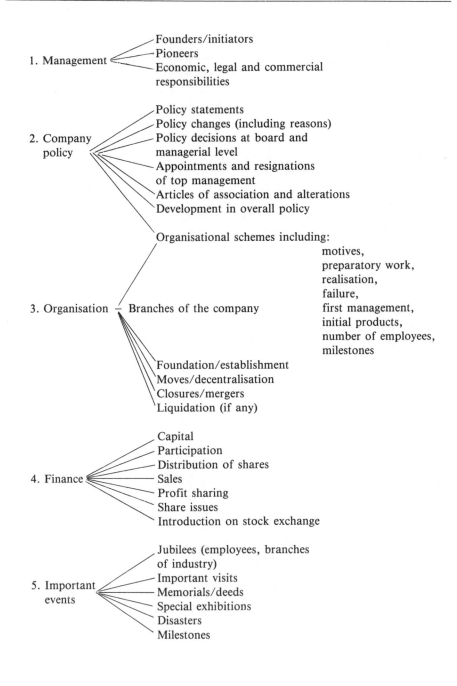

1. Management
- Founders/initiators
- Pioneers
- Economic, legal and commercial responsibilities

2. Company policy
- Policy statements
- Policy changes (including reasons)
- Policy decisions at board and managerial level
- Appointments and resignations of top management
- Articles of association and alterations
- Development in overall policy

3. Organisation — Branches of the company
- Organisational schemes including: motives, preparatory work, realisation, failure, first management, initial products, number of employees, milestones
- Foundation/establishment
- Moves/decentralisation
- Closures/mergers
- Liquidation (if any)

4. Finance
- Capital
- Participation
- Distribution of shares
- Sales
- Profit sharing
- Share issues
- Introduction on stock exchange

5. Important events
- Jubilees (employees, branches of industry)
- Important visits
- Memorials/deeds
- Special exhibitions
- Disasters
- Milestones

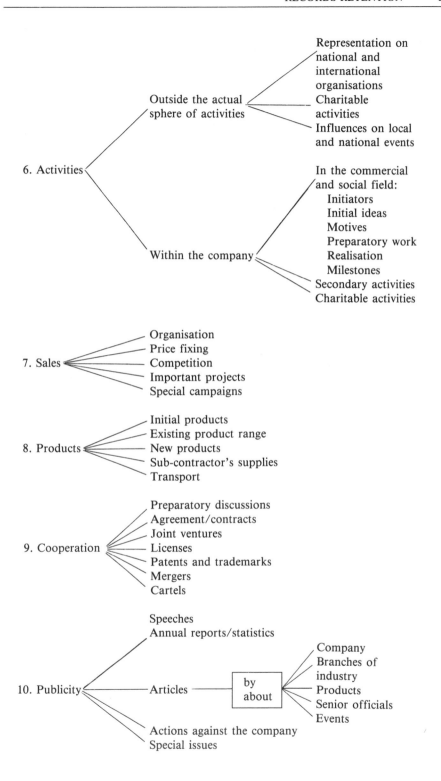

6. Activities

Outside the actual sphere of activities
- Representation on national and international organisations
- Charitable activities
- Influences on local and national events

Within the company
- In the commercial and social field:
  - Initiators
  - Initial ideas
  - Motives
  - Preparatory work
  - Realisation
  - Milestones
- Secondary activities
- Charitable activities

7. Sales
- Organisation
- Price fixing
- Competition
- Important projects
- Special campaigns

8. Products
- Initial products
- Existing product range
- New products
- Sub-contractor's supplies
- Transport

9. Cooperation
- Preparatory discussions
- Agreement/contracts
- Joint ventures
- Licenses
- Patents and trademarks
- Mergers
- Cartels

10. Publicity
- Speeches
- Annual reports/statistics
- Articles — by / about
  - Company
  - Branches of industry
  - Products
  - Senior officials
  - Events
- Actions against the company
- Special issues

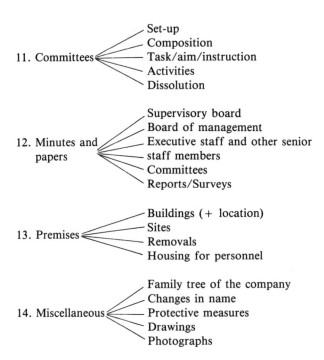

11. Committees
- Set-up
- Composition
- Task/aim/instruction
- Activities
- Dissolution

12. Minutes and papers
- Supervisory board
- Board of management
- Executive staff and other senior staff members
- Committees
- Reports/Surveys

13. Premises
- Buildings (+ location)
- Sites
- Removals
- Housing for personnel

14. Miscellaneous
- Family tree of the company
- Changes in name
- Protective measures
- Drawings
- Photographs

Chapter 4

ARCHIVAL STORAGE OF PAPER RECORDS[1]

1. ARCHIVE AND RECORD REPOSITORIES

1.1. PREMISES

Archive and record repositories should give their contents full protection against fire and water and should be able to control the level of temperature and humidity within their environment. The temperature in the storage area should be around 18°C (65°F).

- The building should be guaranteed to stand at least one hour of fire.
- The air conditioning and ventilation system should be controlled as fire and/or smoke can travel through ventilation ducts and water used for extinguishing a fire may seep into the archive/records store and cause considerable damage.
- A check on the construction of water pipes and electrical installations is recommended.
- The door to the storage area should have a fire resistance of at least one hour and it should also be fitted with high security locks.
- The premises should have as many "clear" areas as possible i.e. no pillars, salient parts of the walls etc. The floor should be very strong and be able to hold 8 kN/m³. The weight per shelf metre is then maximized to 600 N.[2]
- Every floor in the repository should have a work area, equipped with a desk and chair.

The following factors should be considered when planning the construction of record and archive repositories:

- The current quantity of records.
- The annual growth and the annual loss of records (the net growth should be calculated for at least 10 years).
- A limit to the increase in growth based on previous experience (empirically about 10 – 15% of the calculated sum).

1. For microfilm storage see Chapter 7 and for storage of magnetic tape see Chapter 8.
2. $9.81 N = 1 kg$

1.2. STORAGE CONDITIONS

Ideally an air conditioning system should keep all storage areas at a steady temperature not exceeding 18°C (65°F). A lower temperature can be maintained if personnel are not going to work in the area. If the temperature is between 13°C and 18°C (55°F and 65°F), a constant humidity not exceeding 60% and preferably lower should be maintained. If the air is too dry, paper kept in the premises will become brittle and age rapidly. If the humidity figure is too high, moisture will cause damage and the paper will be affected by mould, mildew and other fungi. Some insect pests, e.g. booklice *(pscoptera)* subsist on mildew and fungi found on damp documents and can cause serious damage to paper records.

The air should be kept in continuous motion and where feasible incoming air should be filtered to eliminate 95% of dust particles of 2 μm or more.

Ideally storage areas should have no windows but in all areas direct daylight should be kept to a minimum. Protective blinds or ultra-violet excluding perspex can be fitted to the windows or alternatively ultra-violet absorbing paint can be applied. Fluorescent tube lights fitted with diffusers and effective ultra-violet light filters are also recommended. Newsprint and other inferior paper should be stored in the dark.

1.3. STORAGE AND SHELVING

It is important that, as far as possible, the records are stored in standard size acid-free boxes and that the boxes are labelled in a standard fashion. All but large bound volumes should be stored upright, standing on shelves. Large volumes (about 75 cm or more in height or width) should be stored flat on shelves wide enough to provide maximum support.

The shelving should be made of strong non-combustible material, sufficiently deep to provide full support to the whole width of the standard box size used. The shelves should adjust vertically so that the full height of the box can be accomodated and they should be not more than one metre in length. The top shelf should always be covered to protect the records against dust. For convenience the shelving should not contain more than six shelves.

Air circulation has also to be taken into account and this means that the shelving should not be placed close to the walls nor too near the floor. Any risk of flooding will mean that the distance between the floor and the lowest shelf should be 15 cm. The aisles should be about 80 cm wide. A repository filled with conventional or static shelving will hold 5 – 6 shelf metres per m^2 and with compact or mobile shelving about twice as much.

Even if mobile shelving is chosen, it will be necessary to install fixed shelving covering about 10 – 20% of the storage area to be used for deliveries, sorting, etc. It is also advisable to have a certain number of shelves, wider than the standard measure as many records, including modern accounting records, are larger than standard shelving.

Chapter 5

REPAIR AND CONSERVATION OF PAPER RECORDS

SIMPLE REPAIRS

Paper records are often so badly kept or treated, that they are torn or suffer fibre breaks before reaching the archive. The damage may be considered insignificant but action must be taken as early as possible, if the damage is not going to get worse.

Dry heat and damp conditions are the real enemies of paper. The former causes paper to become brittle and the latter encourages attacks by mildew and mould. Treatment for extensive damage has to be handled by experts. This chapter will only give some simple quidelines as to the methods for removing adhesive tape, cleaning dirty paper, repairing tears, inserting loose sheets, repairing broken covers and dealing with damage caused by damp and insect pests.

1. REMOVING ADHESIVE TAPE

"Scotch Tape", "Sellotape", etc and all other pressure sensitive tapes and their adhesives are difficult to remove. They should never be used on archive material as the adhesive tape damages the paper fibre. Not all types of tape have the same composition and the solvents used by experts are not available commercially and are often highly toxic. Solvents which are available commercially, e.g. "Genklene" should be applied carefully with a small brush in a attempt to loosen the adhesive tape. Force should not be used and if the tape will not come away easily, expert advice should be sought. The sticky brown substance which is left on paper when adhesive tape dries up, should also be removed as its destructive work will have started on the paper fibres. To save the paper and reduce the damage being done, the tape must carefully removed. A piece of cotton dipped in ethyl alcohol (ethanol), i.e. pure alcohol, should be used gently to remove the sticky resin. However, depending on the surface of the paper and the composition of the tape, it is possible that this treatment will not be succesful. In such cases, a very small quantity of acetone or ether (diethyl ether) should be applied. This method is applicable on small areas of damage, larger areas require treatment by a specialist.

2. CLEANING PAPER DOCUMENTS

Initial cleaning should be undertaken using a soft brush to remove surface dirt and debris. Remaining dirt and small spots of skin grease can be removed by using a soft PVC rubber. Great care must be taken not to rub too hard or damage will occur to the paper fibres. Larger grease spots and those emanating from water-soluble colours (colour weak spots) can be removed by washing both sides of the paper with a piece of cotton dampened in a weak soap emulsion, preferably made of mild soap flakes. A check must be made to establish that the writing medium is water-resistant before attempting to clean a document by this method. The liquid mixture must be used sparingly as the paper must not become too wet. When the washing process is finished the paper is placed between two absorbent pieces of board. A piece of weighted wood is placed on top to prevent the paper wrinkling. If there are any acid spots on the paper, cleaning is best left to a specialist, who will use chemicals to clean the document.

3. REPAIRING TEARS

Paper tears must be repaired as quickly as possible in order that further damage can be prevented. Very thin paper, called Japanese paper, weighing only 9 grams/m^2, is used to repair small tears. This tissue is so thin that writing is visible through it and consequently the repair can be done directly onto the text. A vegetable glue[1] is used as adhesive.

A round water-colour or a flat art paint brush is used to spread the glue about 3 mm around the split. Then a large piece of tissue is placed over the damaged area. The paper is then placed between cardboard to dry.

When the glue has completely dried, the tissue is carefully removed by hand, scraping with a sharp knife or scalpel round the edge of the glued area. Finally very fine sand paper of about 300 granular is used to smooth the tissue until the repair is invisible.

Large tears or damaged corners are repaired by using thicker rice paper weighing about 30 grams/m^2. The technique is the same as that for using tissue paper. See figure 1 and 2 (page 38).

---

1. If such a glue is difficult to obtain commercially, it can be made by mixing rice starch and water together, bringing the mixture to the boil and cooking it until it forms a thin porridge. When it is cooled, it is thinned with water until the desired consistency is obtained. Finally, a few drops of a 10 % formalin solution are added.

4. INSERTING LOOSE SHEETS

The loose sheet should be prepared by cutting off a few millimetres from the inside edge since, when it is fitted, it will not be possible to reach the very back of the volume. This stops the front edge of the inserted sheet sticking out. The same kind of glue is used as that for repairing tears. The glue is brushed onto the paper to a width of 3 – 4 mm. The sheet is immediately inserted into position, the volume closed and left to dry for half an hour after which time the sheet is fixed. See figures (page 38).

5. REPAIRING BROKEN COVERS

Usually a special kind of linen is used to repair covers but very high quality paper of 100 grammes weight can also be used as long as the volume does not need rebinding. PVA-glue is suitable but wallpaper paste can also be used. The drying time is very short, about 15 minutes. Large scale damage must be repaired by specialists. See figures 4 (page 38).

6.1. DAMP

Paper records which have been stored in damp conditions are often affected by mildew, mould or foxing. Mildew in its early sages can often be overlooked as it is difficult to see but where damp is evident, mildew must be presumed and action taken.

The first thing to do is to dry the material to a moisture content below 10% so that the mould is stable and can be brushed off without causing damage. The records should then be dry cleaned with a soft brush vacuum in a well ventilated room. Mould spores are toxic and must not be inhaled, so a mask should be worn while carrying out this work. After the drying and brushing, the records should be wiped with cotton wool pads. There is little point in putting cleaned and/or fumigated records back into infected storage conditions so the storage area and shelves should be sterilized by washing/wiping them with standard non-bleach household disinfectant.

If the mould attack is serious, the records should be fumigated. This can be done in one of two ways. Firstly, by placing them in an air-tight cabinet and exposing them to thymol vapour for a couple of hours per day over a period of up to two weeks. 28g of thymol crystals are required to sterilize the contents of a .45 cubic metre cabinet. Secondly, volumes or documents can be interleaved with tissue impregnated with a 5% weight/volume solution of sodium orthophenylphenate at the rate of 1 leaf of tissue for every 5 to 10 pages. The tissue should be left for about two to six months, depending on the extent of infestation. Foxing, the discolouration of paper by reddish brown spots, can also be treated in this way.

6.2. INSECT PESTS

Mould growth often leads to insect attack on records. Several varieties of insect can live on paper records. Such as booklice *(psocoptera)*, silverfish *(thysanura)*, and firebrat. Booklice can live on mildew and mould fungi. Silverfish and firebrats live on paper, glue, paste, leather, etc.

The best way to prevent insect attack is to keep records in the archival storage conditions described in Chapter 4. By eliminating humidity, and therefore, mould and fungi, and dust, insects are denied sustenance. If large scale infestation has occurred, the only solution is a thorough investigation by professional experts. If, however, the infestation is limited to a small quantity of records action can be taken. The records, in the first instance, should be brushed in a well ventilated room to remove all dust, dirt, etc. Then they should be placed loosely in a container in which are placed crystals of paradichlorobenzene (42 g per 105.4 cm^3 of air space) or a dish of chloroform (28 ml per 105.4 cm^3 of air space). The container is then sealed, left for at least two weeks and then opened in a well ventilated area. Once again the storage area involved must be thoroughly cleaned.

It should be noted that one treatment may not be enough to eliminate all the insects as the eggs and pupae of the insects are resistant to insecticides. This means that the records must be watched for at least a year and the fumigation repeated if insects reappear.

A simpler, safe and effective way of destroying insect infestation is to deep freeze the records. Each item should be placed in a polythene bag, sealed after excluding surplus air, and frozen to a temperature below $-30°C$ ($-22°F$) for 36 hours. Most insect life in all its forms, eggs, larvae, etc. are destroyed by this method *but* fungal growth is not affected. To eliminate the danger of condensation forming on the surface when the item is removed from the freezer, it should be immediately taken out of the bag and placed in a cardboard box for twenty-four hours before being returned to its storage position.

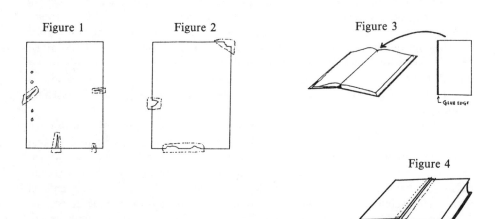

Figure 1

Figure 2

Figure 3

GLUE EDGE

Figure 4

Chapter 6

PLANS, DRAWINGS, MAPS, PHOTOGRAPHS

1. PLANS, DRAWINGS AND MAPS

Plans and drawings often make up an important part of the production records created by a buisness.

1.1. STORAGE

Plans, drawings and maps can either be stored flat in drawers or hung fully supported in special cabinets. They should not be folded. Large plans and drawings can also be wrapped with an acid-free barrier and stored horizontally on shelves, with or without pigeon-hole type boxes. When storing plans and drawings in cabinets, it is essential that the cabinet drawers are not too deep and it is advisable to store only a few drawings or plans in each drawer as otherwise they risk being damaged when they are taken out or put back.

1.2. REGISTRATION

1.2.1. Plans

Plans usually deal with property and the ownership of houses, factories and land. They may show boundaries and the results of land surveys and are important when regulating the transfer of property and wealth and establishing building and town plans.

It is often sensible to use geographical coding when registering plans. Real estate and land registration is often already regulated by national and local government agencies and it is practical to include such registration details in the registration system used by the company.

Whether manual or computer based, registration often consits of a card system, each plan having a card on which information about the creator of the records, the classification, scale, size and date is recorded. Additional items of information can include the county or area, the transfer date to final storage, the plan's condition, the draughtsman or cartographer, and text if any. The cards are then sorted in alphabetical or numerical order following the classification adopted.

Example of alphabetical order

Factory Emerson B 23
Factory Emerson B 28
Lorry no 2
Property no 456
Seahouse no 6
. . .

When non-current plans are transferred to a records centre or archive, their cards also transferred to form a separate card index for plans in the new storage areas.

Changes to, and the sorting of, cards are faciliated in a EDP-system. It is always essential to keep the registration system up-to-date.

1.2.2. Property drawings

Drawings of houses, factories and other buildings are usually best registered by the classification number or code for the property building by building.

Example of drawing registration

Name of firm............................Reg.no...........................
Type of object, real estate..
Address..
Building or part of building.................Type of drawing.................
Drawing no per project.........Drawing date.........Revised code.........
Latest revised date..............Scale...............Format...............
Heading (describing text)...
....
Remarks...
....

The different types of building drawings can be grouped and sorted by function e.g. architectural drawings, constructional drawings, electrical and ventilation installation drawings, etc. They should be numbered within each type of drawing.

Thus an index can be kept by the classification of the property, building by building and according to drawing type. It is also possible to give the drawings running numbers and to store them in numerical sequence. This running number must be included in the classification system. A system with running numbers can be advantageous as unqualified personnel can easily find and replace drawings stored in a strict numerical order.

Even if drawings are stored in numerical sequence, the index will still operate by classification so that, for example, property Brickhouse 1:23, will be followed by Brownhouse 23, etc. If the drawings for Brickhouse 1:23 consist of 13 architectural, 43 constructional, 3 electrical, 4 ventilation, and 3 for the heating system, they will be registered as: A1 – A13, C1 – C43, E1 – E3, V1 – V4 and H1 – H3.

The registration system remains the same if the drawings are microfilmed and kept on microcard (micro-opaque, microprint). An index can be built into the microcard system.

1.2.2. Technical drawings

A product number or code plus a running number can be applied to such drawings and thus form an index. A secondary index may be added to the main one, making it possible to refer to a special order or customer.

Drawings created by consultancy agents should be separated and registered by the name of the consultant and product code or number. Drawings referring to hiring-agreements and standard drawings should be kept apart from other types.

1.3. APPRAISAL, RETENTION AND DISPOSAL

Plans and drawings are generally regarded by companies as being very valuable tools for the administration and management of their business. In a wider context their value is also high. The history of the development of technology and civilization and research into industrial archaeology requires such material. Plans and drawings are important sources of information about former factory sites, etc. Another aspect, of special importance in to-day's society, is that plans can contain information concerning the past dumping or handling of dangerous products or waste, which may severely affect the life of people living in a certain area.

A company may possess many thousands of drawings and plans and so it is essential to control their flow, appraise them and dispose of those which are not vital to any of the interests mentioned above.

The following categories of plans and drawings can be identified:

1. Plans dealing with land ownership, property, town and building planning, pipelines for water and drainage, roads, cables for telecommunication, etc.
2. Technical drawings of processes, flow charts, organisation charts, etc.
3. Building drawings concerning projects and planning, aggregates and details for architectural, facades, and fittings such as windows, doors, staircases, lighting, etc. and equipment such as windows, doors, staircases, light, etc.
4. Residential drawings.
5. Technical drawings of electrical equipment.
6. Technical drawings of machinery (including instruction), aggregates and details of motors, pumps, fans, compressors, machinery parts, trucks, boats, cars, etc.
7. Other production and product drawings.

It is usual to find within these categories original and duplicate drawings not only from the company but also from consultants and other experts.

So long as the buildings are in use, the company's own original drawings and copies from consultants and other experts should be kept. When buildings are empty

and/or are planned to be demolished the following drawings should be retained:
- Main elevation and section drawings so that buildings can be reconstructed
- Drawings and schemes concerning the process techniques involved, both past and present
- Maps and plans relating to the land and area where the factory is or has been situated
- Drawings of machines and products which are important for research into the history of technology
- Drawings of residential buildings which are of interest for research into the history of social development and architecture

2. PHOTOGRAPHS AND CINEMATOGRAPHIC FILMS

2.1. STORAGE

The conditions under which photographs and cinematograph films are recommended to be stored are quite different from those relating to paper, and they should be segregated from other records. Ideally photographs should be copied to provide a security negative and a reference print, although in practice this may have to be restricted to valuable or badly deteriorating photographs and negatives on a cellulose nitrate base. Cellulose nitrate was used as a support for photographic images from the 1890s to the 1950s and is extremely dangerous and damaging to other records. Cellulose nitrate film has a very low ignition temperature and can self-ignite. It also decomposes slowly during natural ageing causing damage to adjacent objects. Nitrate based film should be handled by experts and copied or transferred on to acetate film and the original destroyed. To avoid accidents it should be stored in very cold conditions, in a freezer for example. Glass negatives should be placed in chemically inert paper envelopes and stored in acid- and sulphur-free boxes. Modern gelatin prints and negatives should be placed in chemically inert envelopes, e.g. those made from transparent polyester. The handling of photographs should be kept to a minimum as the sulphides in the human skin are harmful to photographic materials.

A stable temperature between 10°C and 15°C (50°F and 60°F) is recommended for all photographs and film, except colour film for which a lower temperature of between 0°C and 5°C (30°F and 40°F) is advised. A relative humidity of between 40% and 50% is recommended for most paper photographic prints and photograph albums, while between 15% and 30% is recommended for acetate base film. Rapid changes in conditions should be avoided and so provision should be made for gradual acclimatization of photographic materials when they are required for use.

2.2. REGISTRATION

The main demands on a registration system for photographs is that it should

— contain as much information as possible about the photographs
— be possible to use it on small collections as well as large ones
— be flexible, i.e. be able to provide several indexes
— obey the principle of provenance

The registration of photographs should at least include an annotation about its subject and, if they are indexed in such a manner, they are best stored in chronological order. If the collection is of any interest and importance then more substantial information is required. Information to be indexed includes the geographical and organizational origin of the collection or individual photographs (i.e. their provenance), the subject (people or scenery/landscape/environment), the production date, the name of the photographer, technical information (negative or print, black and white or colour, paper print, slide, glass negative, etc.) size, location, when and if it has been published, etc.

A photographic collection usually contains a large number of photographs and in order to aid retrieval it is advisable to have several types of index. These can include:

— Subject
— Place
— Person
— Date
— Name of the photographer
— Technical criteria such as type of prints, type of negative, etc.

Photographs are normally kept together in a photographic collection according to a running number of accession. The registration and cataloguing of cinematographic films must include information about the content/subject, date and technical data. Films can be stored according to the date of production or, especially with advertising films, alphabetically by products. Indexes of products, subjects, places and persons are useful aids for retrieval.

There are no types of video tapes, the modern equivalent of cinematographic film, which are suitable for long term preservation. Currently BCN video tapes are of the best quality for recording, while VCR tapes can not be used for commercial purposes.

Chapter 7

MICROFILM

1. WHY MICROFILM?

There are three main reasons for microfilming records which will not appear in a microform format as normal office routine. The first reason is to safeguard important records, the second is to save space and the third is to multiply access to documents in a cheap and easy way.

When microfilm is an integrated part of office routine, such as the output of computer systems (COM), it should be treated accordingly. The usual rules for the evaluation, retention and destruction of business records come into force.

1.1. MICROFILMING FOR SECURITY REASONS

Microfilm copies of important records are made to ensure against loss of information should the original be damaged or destroyed. The copies should be stored separately, well away from the original, in an controlled environment. At set intervals the film should be checked to ensure that it is still readable and in good condition. This control check can be carried out at random and at intervals of $2-5$ years. If the film is going to be kept long term (around 100 years) then the filming, developing and storage demands are very severe and exacting.

The cost of security filming and the subsequent regular control and storage are low, as the quantity of records to be filmed is generally small.

1.2. MICROFILMING AS A WAY OF SAVING SPACE

Microfilming is often used to save space. When a record series (e.g. invoices) grows very rapidly and the bulk becomes a problem, it is time to decide whether it would be better to keep the information on film instead of paper. Usually such records are due to be weeded and/or destroyed after a few years. The film acts as the working material and is to be kept only for the length of the legal retention period of the series. If it is decided to film short term records, it is recommended that the use of forms is investigated in order to facilitate filming.

Doubts have been raised as to whether microfilming is a really economical way to save space. Legal questions such as the admissibility of microfilm as evidence in court should also be taken into account. The legal position varies from country to country but it is generally held that a minute of the filming has to be recorded.

1.3 MICROFILMING AS A WAY OF DISTRIBUTING INFORMATION

In a company, using many EDP routines, especially where there are large geographical distances between different divisions and/or subsidiaries, it is often easiest to spread information by using microfilm. It is easier and cheaper to send or post microfilm or microfiche instead of paper copies.

2. DIFFERENT TYPES OF MICROFILM

The reason for microfilming records determine the type of film used. When security filming is to be undertaken then silver halide film should be used. When a master film (negative) is to be produced in order that working copies can be made, the film used should be of good quality as 3 − 4 generations can be made from it. Diazo film should be used to produce the daily work copies.

2.1. ROLL FILM

Roll film is inexpensive and its development is relatively simple but this does not mean that roll film is always the best type of microfilm medium. In general, roll film should be chosen when large quantity of records are to be filmed quickly and when one or more rolls of film will be completely filled or if the information is sequentially arranged and no updating is required within the sequence.

The use of roll film also means that the use of automatic search techniques such as blips is also possible. For long term and secure storage only silver halide film is acceptable.

Whether 15, 35 or 105 mm film is chosen will be an individual choice, depending on the type of record to be filmed and the future use of the film. However, the commericial market for 16 mm film is growing and the technical aids, such as readers, are developing very fast. Other techniques which are often supported by EDP, such as analogue or digital storage on discs, are also being developed.

2.2. MICROFICHE

After filming, roll film can be cut and mounted into jackets and duplicated as microfiche. The same result can be produced with a microfiche camera. It is recommended that microfiche is used as a storage media, when the information is structured. The original negative film can be use to make working copies on diazo film for everyday use. Personnel records can be stored in rows so that one row will contain, for instance, holiday records, another health certificates etc., and different types of medical information can be sorted separately (ECG, EEG, laboratory reports, etc.). Information stored in this way can be easily updated and access is good.

Microfiche is

- recommended when multiple copies are required for distribution to various people or places
- very easy to use and to handle
- advantageous as the frequency of exposure does little damage

It should also be remembered that

- the market for microfiche readers is larger and that readers are less expensive than those for roll film
- the cost of sending microfiche by post is lower than that for roll film

Microfiche copying also is simple, quick and cheap. A block or a bar can easily be inserted to prevent access to sensitive or secret records.

2.3. APERTURE CARDS

Aperture cards can be utilized for both 35 mm and 16 mm film or the two combined. The paper section can used for notes about the picture. These can be written in words or code, the latter often being used to ease sorting. Aperture cards are especially practical for drawings and maps. Their advantages are:

- security
- reduced storage space
- originals are left untouched as only copies are handled
- ease of adding information
- ease of duplication
- increased sorting possibilities

3. DECIDING WHETHER TO MICROFILM

Having studied the technical problems and advantages of microfilming, a decision as whether to microfilm or not must be taken. Many questions have to be answered. The frequency of usage and copying has to be considered. The time it takes for personnel to acquire paper copies from the microfilm has to be estimated. The wear on the original records has to be taken into account. Finally, it is essential for a thorough calculation of the cost of the preparation of the records before filming to be ascertained.

When the microfilming is in progress, minutes must be taken and the records being filmed must be marked to guarantee their original order and their authenticity.

When costs are estimated and compared, the following points for conventional storage should be considered: the costs of the premises, the fittings and fixtures and storage equipment, for personnel dealing with the archive and for copying, postage and freight. The following costs should be considered for microfilming: the storage premises, the microfilm readers and printers, the developing, the film, the maintenance of the machines and tools, the copying and postage and the personnel dealing both with the preparation and the management of the film archives.

A detailed evaluation of the suitability and the costs of filming done for reasons of saving space has to contain the following questions:

1. *External form*

   Is it the norm for both sides of the paper to be written on? How large is the volume of records? What kind of paper quality is used? What does the actual text look like? Are originals mixed with copies? Are coloured as well as black and white documents involved? What is the size of the documents? Is this standard? Are the documents so large that the reduction made when filming is so great that paper copies taken from the film will have a scale different from the original?

2. *Storage*

   Are the documents part of a filing system? Are there many drawings? In either of these cases it should be noted that it may be necessary to update the documentation and that may influence the choice of a suitable system.

3. *Retrieval*

   How many retrievals are carried out per week or month. What type of employees do the retrieval? How long will retrieval take and what type of paper copies will be required? What is the length of time that an employee uses a document? This is important when deciding how many microfilm readers and copiers will be required. If employees have to work a lot with paper copies, the film costs increase and it is possible to end up with a growing filing and archival problem.

4. *Space gain*

   This is the most common reason for microfilming. Certain types of document have a very large search and retrieval frequency. If there is no available space close to the person working with them, the documents will have to be kept away from the office. This increases the cost of retrieval and diminishes office efficiency.

When filming is not to be done as part of the working process but some time afterwards, it may require a large series of similar original documents in order to make the costs involved worth while.

Drawings present a slightly different situation. Drawings demand a lot of space and filing cabinets designed for drawings are expensive. It is cheaper to aquire copies from microfilm than from the full scale originals, so the requirement for the latter on quality paper is reduced. Working routines can also be simplified if microfilm copies are used. It is best to microfilm drawings as they are produced or are acquired by a company. If it is decided to microfilm new drawings it should be seriously considered that the old drawings are microfilmed as well, as it is impractical to work with two systems. As it has already been pointed out, it is vital to take into account the reduction in scale. The new digital storage and CAD techniques are being investigated for future use.

The frequency of changes required to be made on drawings is often decisive in the choice of film system as each change means a new copy film. If a jacket system is used the various altered copies can be placed one after the other, and if aperture cards are used, the altered cards can be placed one after each other. It can also be difficult to alter enlarged copies from a aperture card. Copying from a copy continuously reduces the quality of the picture. It is better to alter the original and then microfilm it again.

Good guides must be made to microfilmed archives whether they contain documents or drawings. A register must be maintained to record where certain types of information are to be found on a roll film or on a microfiche. It is possible, when filming with modern techniques, to use blips for this purpose.

3. STORAGE

High quality microfilm must be used if it is required as a medium for preserving records. The original negative (master film) should only be used to make other working copies (diazo copies).

The quality demands of archival film involve

− the film roll
− the camera
− the developing and fixing

Exposed film must be handled according to fixed rules. Master roll film must consist of silver halide film and should be stored separately from paper at a temperature of 11°C (52°F) and a relative humidity of 30%. The air should be unpolluted. Paper and film require to be kept separately as paper creates peroxides which can harden film. Master film requires to be kept in labelled boxes or envelopes which will not harm the film. If archival film is to be used, it has to be gradually acclimatized to room temperature before and after usage.

Chapter 8

MACHINE-READABLE RECORDS

A considerable quantity of contemporary records is generated by a computer. It is thus essential for records managers and archivists to learn how to deal with this kind of record. As it has already been said, records and archive management have to be carried out on all types of records, regardless of their physical form and characteristics. Steps have to be taken and rules have to be established to locate, appraise and deal with machine-readable records.

It is also true that computer techniques are rapidly changing and that it is difficult to keep abreast of present, or to predict future developments. Some new innovations, however, are visible, such as artificial intelligence, the use of mainframes in combination with personal computers (PCs), etc. but other changes will occur.

Input, processing and output make up the information cycle for all computer systems. It can also be generally stated that any information, which can be produced in machine-readable form can also be produced on paper or microfilm.

Machine-readable records have to be treated like all other records and be considered as part of the information flow within a company. Thus they have to be inventoried, and flow charts drawn up. After making an inventory of the system/s, *one* of the problems for the archivist is to decide on the best format and medium for the preservation of the most valuable information for research use in the future.

The present information process operates through the three stages of input, processing and output, but future systems like electronic mail, telefax and others are very different.

INPUT

The information carriers used for input have so far mainly consisted of paper, but this is rapidly changing and microfilm and machine-readable records now form a large part of this input. In some of the EDP-systems, part of the system consists of creating, revising and updating permanent data files and data bases. The input, when it is in the form of another magnetic tape with corrections and updates, is temporary and the files are then called processing or transaction files. Data bases are usually updated via terminals. In a system where data is on paper, the transaction files are analogous to rough drafts and corrections. The important input files created during the processing stages are master files. These consist of data which hold complete and correct information and are, therefore, final versions. A final version may have passed through many temporary processings and so many temporary files may have been used.

OUTPUT

The information carriers used for output can consist of paper and microfilm as well as machine-readable records. There is a difference between the contents of the output of a system, such as printed output which has been collected, sorted and arranged and the contents of the machine-readable records from which the output is derived. Printed output may consist of a list of selected data, while machine-readable records are the only existing version of the data at micro-level. Output which is only visible on terminals is becoming increasingly common. As computers are used extensively by companies for housekeeping tasks, such as payroll functions, accounting, inventories and purchasing, this leads to common types of output data such as bills, renewal notices, accounts, statistical tabulations and narrative reports.

DOCUMENTATION

Documentation is the key source of information about records in a automated system. Without documentation the records are inaccessible. It is also essential that the documentation is available on paper and not only in machine-readable form. The documentation of a system describes its logical design, its purpose, the data entry, the data processing procedure and coding, the software required to operate it, and the types of reports and other output it produces. The program documentation explains the purpose of each computer program, its basic logic, and the function of each instruction or sequence of instructions within it. Technical documentation is of course equally important.

MAKING AN INVENTORY OF MACHINE-READABLE RECORDS

Making an inventory of machine-readable records is just the same as making one for paper records. The purpose of an inventory is to provide information about the creator or the legal custodian of the data file, which may be the division of a firm or the firm itself. It is also useful to record the name of a contact person, who can supply further information about the content and use of the file. It is necessary to know the name of the system or data base. The file should have a title, and other information must be known about it, such as the coding, format, density (bpi), size of the file, etc. It is also necessary to discover the purpose and use of the file, its contents and its arrangement. Information about the input and the output of the file and how it is up-dated is also required. As with other records in an archive, the archivist also requires to know whether there are any restrictions on access or use. A description of the documentation necessary for understanding and using the system is, of course, also essential.

As can be easily understood, surveying machine-readable records in an EDP-system takes time and requires patience and the co-operation of many people within a company.

APPRAISAL

Appraisal of machine-readable records is theoretically similar to the appraisal of information stored on paper or microfilm, but in practice it poses special problems. Due to the growing use of computers, it is not only the information value but also the legal and evidential value that has to be considered.

Evaluating the information means looking at the subject content of the file and finding out the level of aggregation. It will be necessary to decide whether the information will be preserved for the future as summary statistics at a micro-level or as variables. It should be noted that aggregated data can never be reconstituted. The cost of preserving data in a more detailed way has to be matched with its research value. It will also need to be decided in what form the data is to be kept for future preservation – on paper, as microfiche (COM), on magnetic tape, etc. It is also important when appraising computerized data to discover the system for updating the files as the frequency of updating will affect preservation and storage decisions. As has already been stated, the full preservation of both updated and older versions of the documentation is absolutely essential.

It is advisable to set up an archival programme for the preservation of machine-readable records and to ensure that control is established early in the life cycle of the system. The ideal situation includes the presence of an archivist when a system is designed in order that the questions of appraisal, retention and destruction are taken into account at an early stage, but this situation rarely exists.

The majority of machine-readable records in an administrative system are temporary files used for corrections, revisions and extracted output from master files or data bases. These temporary files do not require the major attention of an archivist, who should instead concentrate on master files and data bases. At fixed times it may be necessary to "freeze" the master file or the data base in order to secure the information for future research.

A records creation plan for machine-readable records will look approximately the same as one for non machine-readable records (see chapter 1). Thus it should include the name of the file's legal custodian, the title of system or series, the inclusive dates, and a short description of the content, purpose and use. Other information to be included are restrictions on use and a decision about retention or destruction. If machine-readable records are to be kept permanently, it should be stated when this will occur. If they are to be destroyed, the time for that event should be indicated.

MAKING A GUIDE

A finding aid for machine-readable records is compiled in the same way as for paper records. The content of the tapes will determine how the inventory and the guide are compiled. It is to be remembered, however, that the preservation of the information on the tapes requires technical documentation such as physical information about density, parity etc., information about hardware and software and the structure and organization of the data.

STORAGE

When machine-readable records are to be preserved on magnetic tapes, new tapes should be tested before being used. No tape has an infinite lifespan. Tapes which meet quality standards will probably survive for 20 years, but they will have to undergo regular control checks. The main problems occur with the change of machines and generations. One solution to this problem is to use an exchange format such as the MARC-AMC[1], which is independent of hardware. Preservation demands the use of new tapes, well labelled and the retention of system and program documentation. The label on the tape should provide information about both technical matters and the contents and arrangement of the records.

The storage conditions for magnetic tapes are not the same as those for storing paper or microfilm. The same requirements exist for protection against fire, humidity and water but magnetic tape is inherently unstable and requires exacting environmental control of a temperature between 18° and 20° (64° and 68°F), relative humidity of between 40% and 50% and a minimal fluctuation. The tapes should be stored upright in plastic cases on strong earthed metal racks in a dust free atmosphere remote from sources of magnetic flux. A maintenance scheme should be set up so that the tapes are regularly checked and recopied at annual intervals with rewinding and retensioning carried out at six monthly intervals.

---

1. MARC-AMC, Machine Readable Cataloguing — Archives and Manuscripts Control, see N. Sahli, *MARC for archives and manuscripts: the AMC format.* Chicago 1985

Chapter 9

ACCOUNTING RECORDS

Accounting records form a large part of a company's record holding and are often disposed of as early as financial legislation allows. However, without accounting records the history of a company can not be fully understood.

1. GENERAL BOOK-KEEPING

Book-keeping developed as a means of recording the financial status and transactions of a business in a chronological and systematic way. Book-keeping systems vary from company to company and country to country. One general criterion is that book-keeping should provide an immediate financial overview of a company and the results of its various financial transactions.

It is essential for the archivist, the records manager and the researcher to understand the accounting system of the company with which they are concerned. Such knowledge is essential if the management, production, success of a business, etc. is to be understood. Many researchers have spent months trying to understand the different systems used by companies, how they operated, how they paralleled, overlapped and succeeded each other. Consequently, it is important for the archivist to discover when changes in book-keeping occurred within a company and describe accurately the accounting systems and the records produced by then. One way to understand the system within a company is to follow an invoice through the accounting system, observing where it is recorded and how the records inter-relate and then compile a flow chart of the system. Examples of various stages of book-keeping and the way they inter-relate are included. See pages 60–61.

2. THE DIFFERENT PARTS OF BOOK-KEEPING

2.1 BOOKS OF ACCOUNT

Books of account record the transactions of a business day by day, entry by entry. Similar items, for instance invoices, may be brought together to form one entry. These can be divided into two main groups: *Books of original* entry, where details of transactions are entered chronologically and *Ledgers*, which contain the accounts where information from the original entry books is posted.

2.1.1. Books of original entry

Daybooks – In the early days of double entry book-keeping, transactions were first recorded in a waste book, often called a day book, before being transcribed into a journal

Journals – The journal entries give a detailed chronicle of business transactions. The information contained in each journal entry is posted to the corresponding ledger

Others – Larger businesses have replaced the single book of original entry with separate books of entry, each devoted to a chronological record of a particular transaction e.g. sales and purchase journals, rent books, cash books, bills receivable and bills payable books, etc.

2.1.2. Ledgers

Ledgers record business transactions systematically in columns for different accounts. Information from the original books of account is posted to the ledger, which contains the individual accounts of customers, suppliers, category of goods, venture, type of income or expense, profit and loss, etc.

The main ledger notes systematically the accounting of assets, debts, capital and results (profit and loss). At first it contained column accounts for both people and items but later a settlement-book was introduced for specifying personal accounts with only a collective account appearing in the ledger.

2.2. BALANCE SHEET AND ACCOUNTS

The balancing of the account books, i.e. the production of the final accounts is achieved by the balances of the profit and loss accounts in the main ledger being brought together to form a joint profit and loss account, and the balance from this is transferred to the capital account. The accounts for assets and debts are closed and the balances are transferred to the outgoing balance account, which also contains the balance of the capital account. The balancing of the books means that all the accounts are closed. It is officially done once per accounting year and is the basis of taxation. Internal balancing of the books is often done at shorter intervals, for instance, once a month or once a quarter.

Annual accounts contain profit and loss accounts and a balance sheet with appendices

Profit and loss accounts are statements of income and expenditure of a business during the accounting period

Balance sheets are statements of the assets and liabilities of a business at the end of an accounting period

2.3. ASSISTING/SECONDARY BOOK-KEEPING RECORDS

Personal ledger − all entries concerning customers and suppliers are carried forward from the daybook to the personal ledger, where every customer and supplier has their own account

Stock-book − all entries concerning the purchase or sale of goods are brought forward from the daybook to the stock-book, where every line of goods has its own account

Balance book − all the names of the persons, who have been dealt with during one month, are entered from the personal ledger. The balance book is used as a control to check that all the entries are correctly entered in the personal ledger and the main ledger

Voucher book − lists the incoming and outgoing invoices and is also used as a control

Bills discounted ledger − gives information about the date when bills of exchange and invoices are payable

Income book − is a day-book for profit and income, which is also used as a control

Salary book − salaries are specified in a list, and the lump sum is entered in the daybook and the main ledger. The salary book is thus a verification

Trial balance (rough balance) − a list of all accounts used during the accounting period with their total sums on the debit and credit sides

Expense book (cost book) − is a daybook for expenses which is also used as a control

Further examples of this kind of book-keeping record are the petty cash book, calculation book, price book, order book and promissory note book.

3. THE HISTORICAL DEVELOPMENT

3.1. SINGLE ENTRY BOOK-KEEPING

Originally book-keeping was very simple and business events and transaction were only recorded once in chronological order. The following accounting records were then kept.

1. Daily

a) Daybooks which consisted of a cash book for incoming and outgoing payments and a note of credit purchases and sales
b) Personal ledgers with accounts for customers and suppliers, i.e. accounts receivable and accounts payable ledgers

2. Annually

a) Annual profit and loss accounts
b) Balance sheets

3.2. DOUBLE ENTRY BOOK-KEEPING

Book-keeping then developed into a double entry system where transactions were registered twice, once as a debit and secondly as a credit. This is done in a chronological and systematical order. The following accounting records can be found in this system:

1. Daily

a) In chronological order
  1. Daybooks, which record transactions whether cash or credit, or incoming or outgoing
b) Systematically
  1. Main ledger (personal and item accounts)
  2. Personal ledger (with accounts for customers and suppliers, mainly on credit)

2. Annually

1. Annual profit and loss accounts
2. Balance sheets

Historically several double entry book-keeping systems have existed for example:

The Italian book-keeping system described by Pacioli in the 15th century. The order for book keeping was:

1. Day book (consecutive basic registration)
2. Journal (basic entries assigned to different accounts)
3. Main ledger (personal and item accounts)
4. Assisting books (such as cash-books, etc.)

The French book-keeping system described by de la Porte in 1673 and 1712. The order for book keeping was:

1. Cash-book, day book, purchase and sales book
2. Personal ledger
3. Main ledger (personal and item accounts)

The German book-keeping system was common in the 19th century in Northern Europe. The order for book keeping was:

1. Cash-book and day book
2. Personal ledger, stock-book
3. Summary journal (item accounts)
4. Main ledger (personal and item accounts, lump sums)

The American book-keeping system in the 20th century consists of a column system, which allows registration in a daybook chronologically as well as systematically in columns for different accounts. Intermittent accounts are collected in a joint column. The order for the book keeping was:

1. Column daybook (with columns for accounts)
2. Personal ledger and stock-book
3. Main ledger (item accounts, lump sums)

5. LEGAL DEMANDS

In all countries there are legal requirements concerning book-keeping and accounting records, which determine the types of records which are created, the length of time and manner in which they are kept and whether there are reasons to keep any of them longer than the legal requirement.

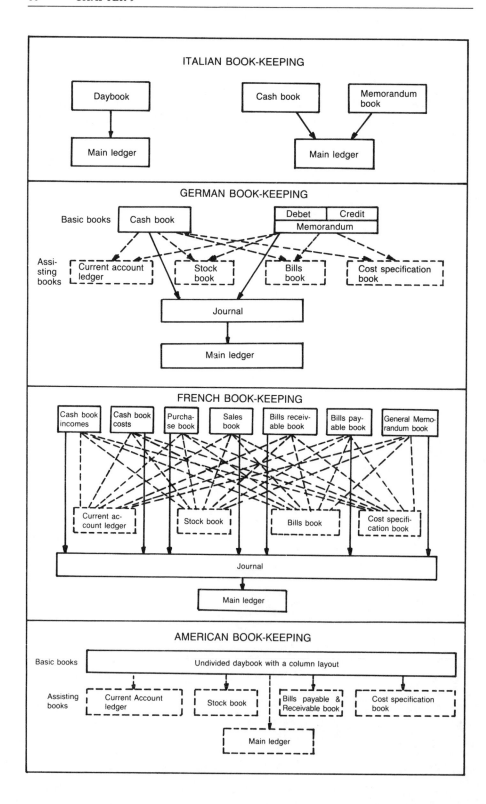

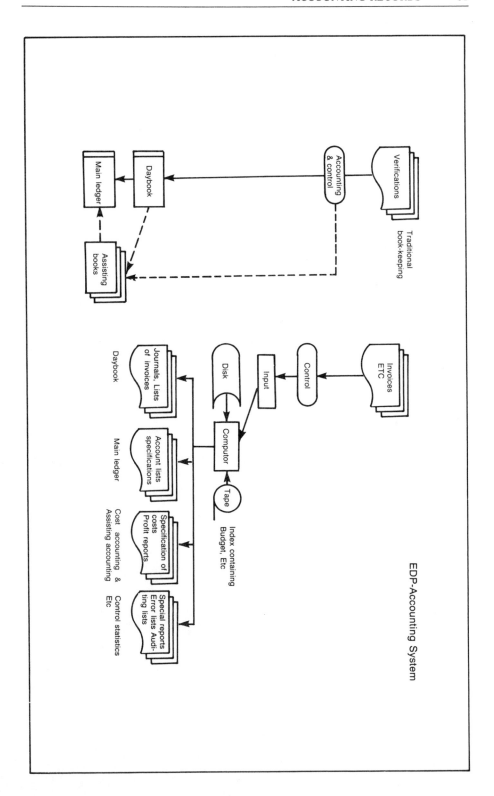

Traditional book-keeping

Verifications → Accounting & control → Daybook → Main ledger

Assisting books

EDP-Accounting System

Invoices ETC → Control → Input → Disk → Computor

Tape

Index containing Budget, Etc

Computor → Journals, Lists of invoices (Daybook)
Computor → Account lists specifications (Main ledger)
Computor → Specification of costs Profit reports (Cost accounting & Assisting accounting)
Computor → Special reports Error lists Audi-ting lists (Control statistics Etc)

Chapter 10

RESEARCH AND THE COMPANY

The interest of companies in research has primarily dwelt in areas where the results have led to practical applications to the development of the companies concerned. The results of such research have mainly been descriptions, analyses and theories concerning the processes, which influence the development, planning, administration, financing and management of businesses. The theories of organisation and systems, economic models and analysis have become important aids to the top management of modern business.

Within this context, historical links have been very small or non-existent. Recently, however, a wider understanding of the historical perspective within economic and political research has been visible. This means, that interest in company records has increased and that new questions and topics of research are of importance.

THE OLD VIEW

The type of historical research that, so far, has involved businesses – often as anniversary publications written by economic historians – has to a great extent viewed the company as a closed unit. Questions and problems concerning leadership and management structures have played an important part in these publications. The company is viewed as a closed system and the analysis primarily deals with events within this system. Outside factors, such as legislation, changing markets, new processes of production, etc., are dealt with in so far as they have an impact on the system, and the resulting history shows how the company as an organisation reacted and responded to these factors. This kind of research, centred on the company, has been built up as a result of technocratic tradition, which in its most pronounced form describes companies as mechanically closed systems.

This approach to research produces the following considerations:

– what distinguishes this branch of trade from others
– what typical features of its branch does the company demonstrate
– what features of the company are unique within its branch

In order to fulfil this type of research, the records to be retained as being of historical value relate to senior management, the organisation and technical aspects of the business. Other records which shed light on the running of the company or its management are only kept selectively.

THE NEW VIEW

This technocratic viewpoint has increasingly been overtaken by another view. Companies are seen as a part of a whole, one jigsaw piece among many, which, when fitted together, form a picture of society. According to this humanistic tradition, the organisation is looked upon as a naturally open system interrelating with its surroundings. This view has also a strong and obvious connection to the discussion concerning environmental and employee care. This research has raised new questions which require to be answered. Interest is shown in such areas, as the way in which individuals are affected by company policy, the continuous interactions between people and organisations and the internal or external reasons for change. Frames of reference and patterns of contact are required to be studied. Thus, when company records are evaluated, it is necessary to have the perspective of the individual and society in mind.

Questions relating to individuals

– the position of every person within the company, group, department or section
– the function and tasks of every department, group or person
– the way different tasks are undertaken

The company chairman, the managing director and the executive staff plan the production, development and policy of the company. Generally, departments which are in charge of the financial, legal and internal management, surveys and research projects are controlled by the above mentioned group of people. It is recommended to keep the records created by this management level.

In the future, due to increased participation by personnel, it will be essential to also retain records outside the senior management level. This increased participation is being created by new forms of management and widening democracy.

QUESTIONS RELATING TO SOCIETY

Three areas are to be distinguished

– company policy
– company actions and management
– company personnel

Company policy can be determined by the minutes of board meetings, management instructions, organisational plans, planning records, company methods and techniques, minutes of important conferences and meetings and specially commissioned surveys. Through these records it is possible to glean pieces of information, which will reveal the first years of a company's existence and its development, management, offices and premises over the years. Executive correspondence often reveals information about the reasons behind the decisions that led to changes in production, trade or marketing.

The proceedings of a company are registered in many different records, some of which have a permanent value, such as annual reports, research reports, some statistical reports, product descriptions, service and maintenance agreements, descriptions of vital production processes, important press releases and some PR-material.

As far as accounting records are concerned annual balance sheets and accounts and all ledgers, plus a sample of book-keeping records, such as those for cash, stock and salaries, should be kept. Routine accounting records such as preliminary accounts, routine reports and correspondence are of less interest. If the administration of the company is to be studied, a small sample will enable several thousand routine transactions to be investigated.

The documentation about the personnel of a company often deals with social and economic conditions. Records concerning salary negotiations and agreements, which emanate from company and personnel associations and clubs, are of interest. Rules and bye-laws about employee participation are vital source material, as are reports and investigations about the attitudes and contributions of employees and their working conditions and environment. Records with a personal touch such as speeches, press cuttings, articles, letters and diaries should be selectively preserved.

Researchers of the new school request records that are centered towards the company, but they will also bypass this frame in order to get a wider perspective of the mutual co-ordination and influence that occurs between the company and its surrounding environment and society.

The researcher's view may also be expressed according to functions and activities of the company. The following system has been formulated by an economic historian[1]. The records of a company to be preserved are those containing information about:

1. The ownership and interest of the owners

A firm's records are undoubtedly the best means of revealing a change of ownership and the balance of power between owners, a change which may have altered the policy and the development of a firm. The changes in ownership must be surveyed.

2. The establishment, construction and development of a company

There is growing interest in discovering how large business organisations (multinational companies) have grown and functioned and how they have been managed. What circumstances result in an organisation with a strong centre with several dependent divisions? Is it better to have a less strong central organisation with independent divisions which can make their own decisions? Information concerning internal discussions about organizational and administrative problems are of great value.

---

1. Quoted with the consent of Professor Rolf Adamsson, see Gallra rätt published by NLA, Karlstad 1986, page 35 – 40.

3. The sales organization

The sales organization might be subordinate to point 2). What is the role of independence, the ability to take initiatives and of aggresiveness? To what degree are these characteristics alternatives to co-operation and a sharing of the market between independent businesses? Does the competence of management lie within production and marketing?

4. Company results

The printed report of the annual results of a company is adapted to the legislation of each country but they are often not informative. There is more information to be found within a company's records. It is important, for instance, to discover the relationship between income and expenditure, if the efficiency of a company is to be revealed.

5. Production policy

This means more than a list of the products. Questions about working processes are linked to environmental problems and the related debate and to their role in present society. How do changes in technical solutions affect the working conditions of employees? What training is required when technology is changed? Simple innovations have often affected a company and its employees more than elaborate ones. Information about such innovations are found in a company's archive.

6. Personnel

Questions about salaries, working conditions, recruitment, the stability of employment within a business sector or within a company and promotion prospects are subjects, which are being studied more and more.

7. The local environment

It has become more and more important to discover the effect that a company has within its geographical location. Why is a company situated where it is? How important is it in the local community, district and region?

DESTRUCTION OF RECORDS

THE WEEDING OF SENSITIVE RECORDS

It is not uncommon for companies to believe that records which might be looked upon and embarrassing to or sensitive for the business should be destroyed. Such destruction implies that too much consideration is taken to subjective and shortsighted evaluations. Destruction should be carried out in such a way as to remove records with as little infringement as possible in the overall quality of the information. Destruction is always risky as it may lead to a transformation or suppression of reality, when certain pieces of information are withdrawn. It is impossible to decide ever-lasting rules as to which records of any given company will be worth keeping for posterity. A company and the society in which it functions are constantly changing and this is reflected in the company's policy and management – and thus in its archives.

There have been cases where a company has acted according to current legal regulations concerning the destruction of records but these regulations have subsequently been altered. The company has then been requested to provide information or evidence about what it once did and has had to face unforeseen costs in searching out the required information from other sources. Such cases affect decisions as whether to keep records or to dispose of them.

SELECTION

GENERAL STATEMENTS

It is not possible to meet every researcher's demand for access to information. Due to the constraints of storage space, it is often the case that a selection or sample has to be made, and there are several methods and techniques for doing this.

When the object is to describe the daily routines and day-to-day management of a company, it should be understood that a small sample will reveal only certain sections of work undertaken. In order to obtain continuity, the selection has to be carried out from the records of each year. The sample has to be large enough to make sure that normal every day transactions will be covered. It is, therefore, unwise to choose letters to and from national correspondents from the correspondence series, or to single out days with unusually small or large purchases from the sales series, when compiling a sample which is supposed to cover a long time span. It is advisable to make sure that the selection is related to the same days and in principle cover the same type of transaction.

Once rules are established for sampling they must always be followed.

EXAMPLES OF SAMPLING METHODS

One method is to make a representative sample by retaining records from only one year or one month within a records series: e.g. within the period 1920 – 1950, to keep the records from the years 1921, 1931, 1941, 1951 or the month of December for each year.

Some statistical and regional methods that are applicable to government records cannot be used for company records due to the diverse content of company archives and the lack of an even geographical spread. Insufficient knowledge of existing company or business archives and their contents can also be an obstacle in the use of many sampling methods.

SUMMARY

When planning to deal with a company's records where no records management plan or archival system exists, it is advisable to take the following steps:

- get to know the organisation of the firm thoroughly
- make an inventory of the records and describe their content and function
- make a decision as to which records *may* be destroyed/weeded including the date, and which *must* be preserved
- prepare a guide to the records which are to be preserved permanently

A more advanced method of records management also includes building up and using a filing/classifications system.

A filing/classification system can be based on

- numbers (100 for economy, 200 for personnel, etc.)
- letters (Ec for economy, P for personnel, etc.)
- both numbers and letters (E 1 for economy, P 2 for personnel)

The system must always be accompanied by a classification key and indices.

The classification of plans and drawings can be based on

- geographical references
- a numerical system
- a code number system

To file documents means to arrange them in a fixed order according to the filling/classification system in use. This filing is usually done in the office. When the files are full, it is necessary to transfer them or some of their contents (for instance those older than 10 years) in order to make room for current papers. This means that some documents are transferred to an intermediate or final repository. The documents are put in boxes, labelled with their classification code (100, Ec, E 1), dates (1970 – 1975) and name of the record series (Files – F 1). This arrangement is carried out according to a set plan (e.g. the records creation plan). This work must be carried out regularly.

Photographs must be filed or registered with information about their date, place and subject matter; cinematographic films must also be accompanied by technical notes.

Microfilm records can be preserved either as

- roll-film
- microfiche/jackets
- aperture cards

When choosing a system the costs must be evaluated. It must be known whether the reason for microfilming is

- security
- distributing information

- COM-technique
- space saving

Information produced by computer processing contains

- basic documentation
- input data
- system and program documentation
- output data

It is important to assess their relationship and their informational value.

The legal requirements for record retention usually involve

- the period of the accounting year
- the retention period for financial records
- the selection of records required in judicial actions (e.g. the incorporation documents of a company, purchases/sales of property, property documents etc.)

It is also necessary to establish which records are admissible as evidence in court as microfilm.

Historical research has increasingly abandoned the perspective of the firm as a closed unit, whose records can only be used to write an anniversary publication. To view the history of the company and its place in its geographical and economical environment raises questions and poses problems, which are related both to the individual and to the society.

However valuable some records series are, their sheer volume can give rise to such storage problems (e.g. certain financial records) that they can only be preserved in sample form.

Sampling methods can be based on

- typical examples (items)
- typical years

Regional and statistical sampling methods can not generally be applied to business records.

APPENDIX

RECORDS TO BE PRESERVED FOR POSTERITY

The following alphabetical list of records, no matter in which form they have been created – paper, film and magnetic tape, etc. – should be preserved for posterity. This list is not exhaustive.

It should be noted that the name given to a type of record or document can vary between companies and countries.

Accident statistics (annual)
Accounting plans
Acquisition papers (takeovers)
Administrative correspondence (policy only)
Amalgamation records
Annual accounts
Annual general meeting minutes
Annual reports
Apprenticeship indentures
Architectural drawings
Articles of association
Assignments
Audit reports

Balance sheets (audited)
Bills payable and bills receivable books
Board meeting minutes and related papers
Board reports
Bond documents
Building plans including those for services
Bye-laws

Committee (various) meeting minutes and
    related papers
Commodity indices
Concessions
Construction plans
Consultancy agreements and contracts
Contract documents
Contract registers and/or lists
Conveyancing documents
Correspondence – directors and managers
Customer registers and/or lists

Debenture trust deeds

Directors' contracts
Discount registers and/or lists

EDP-system and program records
Employee health care records
Employment contracts

Founders' family, etc. papers

Health and safety records

Industrial safety records (a sample)
Insurance policies if they list buildings, plant
    or machinery
Internal circulars and instructions (a sample)
Inventories (for buildings, plant, machinery or
    other property)
Investment plans and calculations

Job studies

Leases
Ledgers
Legal agreements
Legal proceedings papers
License agreements
Liquidation papers
Loan contracts

Machinery plans
Machinery registers
Management meeting minutes and related
    papers
Manufacturing reports
Memorandum of association
Merger papers
Mortgage agreements

Nominal ledgers

Order lists (a sample)
Organisational schemes and plans

Partnership agreements
Partnership meeting minutes
Patents
Pension and staff benefit scheme records
Pensioners social records
Personnel records
Photographs of staff, premises, products, etc.
Plant drawings
Plant registers
Press cuttings
Price lists
Product manuals
Product registers
Production reports
Productions statistics (annual)
Profit and loss accounts
Project summaries, documents and minutes
Promissory notes
Property plans
Property registers
Property sale and purchase documents
Property valuations
Purchase ledgers
Purchase reports and statistics (annual)

Recruitment records (a sample)
Registration certificates
Research reports

Safety reports
Salaries books
Sales brochures
Sales contracts (a sample)
Sales ledgers
Sales statistics (annual)
Security documents
Service documents
Share and stock documents
Share and stock registers
Staff contracts
Staff lists
Statutes
Stock books
Suppliers registers and/or lists
Supply contracts

Tax assessment documents
Technical documentation
Tenancy agreements
Time and motion studies
Title deeds
Trade mark documents
Trade name papers
Trade Union agreements, arbitration and
    negotiation records
Training schemes (a sample)

Valuation certificates
Valuations of buildings, plant, machinery, or
    other property
Vouchers (a sample)

Wages books